PUT THE MAGIC BACK INTO YOUR BUSINESS

Nine Management and Leadership Skills

A FABLE BY

JIH MIN CHENG
GRACY YAP

Put the Magic Back into Your Business

Nine Management and Leadership Skills

Text Copyright © 2020 Jih Min Cheng & Gracy Yap

Illustration Copyright © 2020 Michael Cheng

ISBN-13: 9781653801640

All rights reserved. No part of this book may be reproduced, stored in a retrieval system, or transmitted in any form without the prior permission of the publisher, except for brief passages in a review by a book reviewer.

Printed in the United States of America

Dear Readers,

The idea for this book came about during Jih Min's career in shopping mall management. He encountered many interesting scenarios where issues could have been resolved if the parties involved exercised certain management and leadership skills and communicated their intentions clearly.

This book attempts to distil Jih Min's experiences into core life skills that can be learned by everyone interested in improving their management, leadership, and communication skills. Dive into a magical kingdom of animals from the air, land and sea. How these animals as characters conveying moral lessons skilfully navigated the journey of life by applying these core skills. Over nine chapters, the skills are explained clearly through fables as each skill is meant to be discussed and practised by the reader in a fun and engaging environment.

Learning a skill is the first step, recalling the skills learnt and practising until you master these skills and make it a part of your life, is a goal of this book.

From the Authors

TABLE OF CONTENTS

Chapter 1: Preparation Is Key 1

Chapter 2: Empathy Is Your Friend 3

Chapter 3: Open and Trusting Relationships 5

Chapter 4: Crunching Numbers 7

Chapter 5: Flexibility Wins the Day 11

Chapter 6: A Listening Ear 13

Chapter 7: Have an Inquiring Mind 16

Chapter 8: Decisiveness 18

Chapter 9: Win with Strategy 20

Epilogue – What's Next? 21

Adult Coloring Pages 22

Reflection 32

About The Authors 35

CHAPTER 1: PREPARATION IS KEY

Honey Bee buzzed with excitement. She's been as busy as a bee since morning. No, weeks ago. Today's the day. She checked that everything is in order and once again put on her reading glasses and glanced at the attendance list. The meeting delegates were about to arrive from different parts of the Universe to Magical Kingdom Hotel in this sleepy hallow. It is set to be the largest congregation of sea, land and air animals and insects in the organization. Honey Bee would have given up everything to meet Penguin. Yes, he's cool and dashing!

She checked the agenda on the Notice and ticked that off on her To Do list. She checked her electronic devices and tablet. Sometimes it's wonky in an environment that defied gravity. She looked at the tenancy contracts. Marvelous Studio had just opened a boutique store in the hotel, just doors away from Disnie and Hasbrow. Or was that the lot vacated by Disnie?

Now her wings glistened with sweat in the bright sunlight from all the hustle and bustle. Anchor tenants that attract traffic are so important. It's a win-win for both landlord and tenant; the last thing you want to deal with is a tenant who defaults on rent. Honey Bee flew around to do a final round of inspection. To her dismay, the new shop lots still had work in progress and dust gathered on the hoarding boards. And, horror of horrors, the workers left their footprints along the walkway. What is the CEO going to say? She shuddered nervously.

She flew towards Giraffe, the Marketing Director of Marvelous shop lot. "Hey, do you need help for any cleaning?" she asked. "Nah, everything is under control. Don't worry," Giraffe sauntered off nonchalantly. Honey Bee felt uneasy. She's got this funny feeling that something was amiss.

"Welcome delegates to SEAL Conference" holographic banner in iridescent white really stood out and made her heart sing. Very soon, she'd be busy welcoming the delegates arriving in their flying pods and sea pods. All except Eagle who wanted to make a grand majestic entrance. Honey Bee had prepared trays of lovely rainbow colored fairy cakes and the finest teas to delight the meeting delegates and her co-workers.

Her feelers started quivering. A message beeped. The CEO's PA has transmitted a message that the CEO, the mighty Lion, would inspect the Magical Kingdom Hotel and signages in 30 minutes. Suddenly Honey Bee heard a loud thud. Cat had arrived and was playfully jumping around the mass of hoarding boards. He accidentally toppled a large board over the railings and it almost hit Giraffe who came out for some fresh air. Giraffe saw red as the hoardings disintegrated into a huge cloud of dust, and he started coughing. Everyone started panicking, as the inspection was merely minutes away.

It's show time for Honey Bee! She's well prepared for contingencies. She mobilized her army of worker bees to clear and clean up the mess. Then she called her interior designer team to put up drapes to cover an ugly shop front. She used to be a total failure in crisis management years ago. Experience is a good teacher. And more attention must be placed on Workplace Safety to prevent casualties.

Moral: Be helpful to your co-workers.

Management Skill 1: Nothing like over preparation. Be prepared for the worst. Preparation is Key.

CHAPTER 2: EMPATHY IS YOUR FRIEND

"Your hotel is so spick and span. I cannot find any food crumbs on the floor. I'm starving!" Rat wailed.

Dog sighed and squinted at the tenancy agreement in front of him that Rat intends to breach. Rat is in the scavenger business and he has no business if he cannot hunt for food. So in dire straits, he decided to cut his loss. Rat is living on a prayer. He is at his wits end. Sometimes prayers work miracles.

As it's the festive season with jingle bells ringing and halls decked with boughs of holly, how could Dog be nice to Rat and emerge victorious in the form of an amicable arrangement? His head would roll if he plays Santa Claus. Just then, a knock sounded outside his door. A burly Pig chef almost crashed into his tiny crammed office like a bull in a china shop. Pig huffed and puffed and squealed, "Sir, we have a problem." Dog slammed his forehead with his paw and said, "Oh no, not again! Give me solutions, not problems!" "Sir, we don't have enough walk-in customers today at the restaurant. So now we have too much leftovers. Looks like we are going to be penalized by Mr Lion CEO for breaking the no wastage rule." Pig shivered as he imagined the frightening face of his furious CEO.

"Wait a sec. You said we have leftovers?" Dog inquired. "That's a good problem! Rat here will take care of it. Rat will be delighted to help you solve your problem." A glint appeared in Rat's beady eyes. He scampered to his feet and saluted Dog. "Aye aye, Sir. You've just saved my business. I can't thank you enough." He ran up the bridge of Dog's nose and pecked him on his forehead. Dog blushed a deep red. "Ahem, it's ok. Friends should look out for each other. I'm glad you won't starve anymore and can resume your business. ... Which brings us back to your tenancy agreement. Now that you have a solution, I'll consider that you will continue paying rent." Pig squealed with delight that Dog managed to save his skin, and Rat teared for joy that he won't ever go hungry again. Soon a memorandum was beamed on a gigantic screen to the hotel staff that a new Recycling Program for Food Waste would be put in place at once with Rat as the officer-in-charge of this initiative.

Moral: Be nice to people. Every dog has its day.

Management Skill 2: Put yourself in your customer's shoes. Be empathetic and find a solution that's mutually beneficial to everyone. Sometimes a genius is born when you challenge norms.

CHAPTER 3: OPEN AND TRUSTING RELATIONSHIPS

Penguin sipped his Pina Colada and dipped his flappers into the sea. He loves his mobile lifestyle. It's fabulous, so freeing not to be in a 9 to 5 routine. Every day is different, and routines are boring. Yes, he works remotely and he makes sure he checks his messages every now and then to be available 24/7 for his team. Everyone wants a piece of him. Penguin pours his heart and soul into his business 100 percent. He doesn't want to be mediocre. He wants to be outstanding. It's difficult to get a day's break away from work.

Today he is worshipping the sun and sea on Pebble Beach, while devouring a book on his Kindle Reader on Great Customer Service. Out of the corner of his eye, he was acutely aware that a bikini clad Miss Piggy was worshipping his six-pack bod. He adjusted his sun shades and pretended not to notice.

His flappers started to vibrate and a call came in from the Magical Kingdom Hotel. "Where are you, Penguin? It's your turn to present at the SEAL Conference in 15 minutes!" a voice shrieked on the line. It's Honey Bee, the conference manager. OMG! The big meeting had slipped his mind! "I'll be there," he calmly replied. Splash! He summoned his sea pod and off he went. How nice if he had the super hero ability to teleport! Thank goodness he didn't need a change of clothes and always look well dressed as the Emperor Penguin.

With his dashing good looks, Penguin's charisma has won him a wide circle of friends and a growing fan club. He practises an open door policy. Well, technically there are no doors in the ocean. Female birds in particular, like to hang around him and ask him for advice to their pressing problems. He's always ready to lend them a listening ear, often until the wee hours of the morning. He never turned anyone away, giving everyone a chance to air grievances. In this way, he has cultivated open and trusting relationships, the magic ingredient for his business that keeps clients coming back. For a great customer experience. And today, his time management went out the window because he was mentoring this seagull who has lost his confidence to fly. Sh** happens. It's on days like these that Penguin is grateful for his sea pod. It brings him everywhere; to the ends of the earth.

Moral: Never turn away anyone who needs help. Offer them a listening ear.

Management Skill 3: Tear down walls. They divide us. Develop open and trusting relationships.

CHAPTER 4: CRUNCHING NUMBERS

It's the day of the annual performance review meeting. The whole management team at the Board room waited for Mr Lion CEO to start the meeting. These reviews were nerve wrecking affairs in the past, and it promises to be the same this time round. It's so quiet in the conference room that you could almost hear a pin drop.

The boss Mr Lion CEO is a stern taskmaster, and brooks no nonsense and excuses. One mistake and he will chew his manager up.

All his senior management team were seated at the conference table, waiting in trepidation. Honey Bee, Penguin, Shark, Dog, Chimpanzee, Eel, Dolphin, Cat, and Eagle. They sat eyeing each other, not knowing what to expect. Honey Bee ogled at the handsome Penguin and felt her heart miss a beat. She's finally able to set her eyes on this handsome dude and felt like her heart was going to burst any minute. Ever the workaholic, Penguin seemed oblivious to the flirting as he checked his flappers for incoming messages.

Just then, Mr Lion CEO flicked his golden mane and made a grand entrance into the room. He roared his greetings to his team.

The first item on the agenda was a review of the past year's performance numbers. Lion called upon Chimpanzee, the CFO, who has a head for numbers to present.

Chimpanzee quickly rattled off the numbers:

100,000 people moved through the doors of the Magical Kingdom Hotel every day. 50,000 walked past the shops at the foyer. 10,000 walked into the shops. 5,000 people bought an average of $100 from those shops. Which means $500,000 daily sales were transacted by the shops.

And 10% of the sales was for rent payable to the owner. Which meant $50,000 in daily rental income from the shop tenants in Magical Kingdom Hotel.

Mr Lion CEO roared. "That's not good enough. We only have 10% of guests in the hotel walking into the shops. That is unacceptable.

And a 50% sales conversion rate, while it may look good, is pathetic considering the average sale is only $100 per transaction." Lion true to his predator nature, wanted a lion share.

He then asked each of his management team for their feedback.

Honey Bee was the first to speak up. "Mr Lion Sir, it's because of the construction of the new hotel wing that disrupted the traffic flow to the shops. Once the new wing is open, traffic will go back to normal." Bee did her PESTEL survey study and sounded confident.

Penguin straightened his tuxedo and replied, "Mr Lion Sir, we don't have enough transport to bring visitors across the galaxy to visit the hotel. I suggest we build our own spaceships and transport visitors to the hotel. And build a space port to dock these spaceships."

Shark spoke next, "Mr Lion CEO, out of 10,000 applicants for the new hotel jobs, we only selected 1,000 to work. Shall we entice the other 9,000 to buy something from the shops before they leave the hotel? I will make it my job to make sure they do it. If not, I will crush them with my jaws. Oops, excuse me Sir, I mean I will encourage the shops to give them discounts."

Dog barked next, "CEO Sir, I would like to suggest starting a customer loyalty programme for all the shoppers to take part. When they visit the shops and buy something, they will be rewarded with stars. The more stars they accumulate, the more attractive the gifts they can redeem, like redeeming a space flight to the next Galaxy."

Eel spoke next. "Mr CEO, I suggest giving some incentives to the shop tenants to offer a package deal for visitors, so sales conversion can improve. And you can also offer the tenants a concessionary rent for the first three months of the hotel opening to show our hotel's appreciation for their patience during the development of the new wing."

Dolphin pointed out intelligently, "Mr Lion CEO, why don't we ask our visitors and tenants and get their opinion? That way we can get 100,000 opinions a day."

And Cat purred, "With the new AI tool I'm developing, we can quickly analyze all the opinions and provide real time insight to the Management. "

Eagle screeched, "I can use my long distance hi-ray to see the patterns forming and hot spots of traffic, and give an aerial and big picture feedback."

Chimpanzee grunted, "Based on my calculations after hearing my esteemed colleagues' feedback, we have to spend another million units of Magical Kingdom Hotel currency. What say you, Mr Lion CEO?"

Lion was flabbergasted. He had expected his management team to be wimps. At last year's review, none of them dared to speak up. He had the floor all to himself. Secretly he was proud of his team. He had enrolled them into a management training program the previous year. The trainer had a unique way of training his team. He used fables and stories to train them. This person is a human from the planet Earth. He did not come cheap, as Earthlings are very rare in the Universe. The CEO had to approve the costs for spaceship travel and hibernation allowance as the Magical Kingdom Hotel is located many thousand light years away from Earth. Truth be told, he was hired because of the beautiful female co-trainer he brought along. But he was worth every penny spent.

After a gruelling few hours, the review meeting ended. As the team started moving toward the door, Mr Lion congratulated them on a job well done. He stuck a heart-shaped sticker on each member of his team, to show his love and affection.

When they left the room, Mr Lion CEO quietly smiled to himself. He tapped an invisible button on his paw, and out sprang a hologram. Or rather 9 holograms. Each hologram showing each of his management team. Going about their daily work. Unknown to his team, the heart-shaped sticker is a camera device that captures the images and actions of his team as they go about their work.

For Mr Lion's motto is: "In God we trust. All others need to be monitored closely in real time." How could Mr Lion CEO be the CEO of The Magical Kingdom Hotel if he cannot control his team's every action and thought!

Moral: Big or small, every contribution counts.

Management Skill 4: The CEO must always be on top of things.

CHAPTER 5: FLEXIBILITY WINS THE DAY

Rooster is the assistant to Eel, the Director of Leasing. He adopts a take it or leave it attitude with prospective tenants who want to negotiate the terms of their agreement.

Rooster crowed loudly to his prospective tenants, "This agreement is standard and is the best deal you can get. You cannot change any clause inside. Even if you want to change, I will not allow it." He wanted to impress Mr Lion CEO, by being tough and firm and not giving way.

Eel, on the other hand, is a savvy deal maker. Even the most impossible of deals she could secure for the Magical Kingdom Hotel. Though Eel is good looking in a slippery sort of way, she did not just rely on her good looks to get the deals done. Her secret to closing impossible deals? She knows the terms of the agreement like the back of her body[1] and is able to move flexibly and nimbly in the sea of words and images. The modern agreement is crafted in a hologram, where all sorts of three dimensional words, images, and videos come alive upon a slight twitch of Eel's body. So unlike the archaic paper and word based documents of the past.

Eel was concerned about Rooster's arrogance and inflexibility. She had already received many complaints from potential prospects which the company has been cultivating for many years. All her work would go down the drain if she did not take action. Terminating Rooster's employment was not an option, as he is the brother-in-law of Mr Lion CEO.

---

[1] Well, grammatically it should be 'the back of her hand' but as an eel has no hands, we ask the reader to allow us to exercise our artistic license.

So Eel devised a game to train Rooster on the finer points of negotiating agreements. She wanted to encourage Rooster to change his attitude while not making him feel offended.

She structured her game as a song. From the tenants' perspective.

"I want my shop to be easily configurable in good times and bad times. I want the flexibility of renting some space to my business associates if my business slows down, so I'm not sad. I don't want to keep asking permission from the owner to change a single screw. I don't want to be tied down to a long-term relationship with no hope of leaving, it's not cool. I want every cost item borne by me to be estimated and to cap the increase in costs at a reasonable rate. Don't take me for a fool. Fairness is my mantra. I don't want rents to escalate into outer space. I want to have the flexibility of renegotiating the agreement when the market turns against my business, as we are all in this together. Do not abandon me for a few bucks extra."

Eel got Rooster to sing the song together, where he went off key. They sang, danced and had a ball. After numerous fun practices, Rooster got his 'aha' moment and began to change his attitude to see the point of view of his tenants. He still needed to maintain the position of the owner, but very few things in life are non-negotiable. He got to enjoy his work, his prospective clients liked him, and started referring business. Together with Eel they became a formidable team and unstoppable.

Moral: Make the opponent your friend. Nothing is impossible.

Management Skill 5: Flexibility is essential to solving problems. Just as water can find a way round a huge mountain, so will flexibility find a way around thorny issues.

CHAPTER 6: A LISTENING EAR

It's that time of the year when the shop tenant negotiates with the owner to renew the agreement for another year. Rabbit is keen to stay on for another year in the same place, as he has generated good sales from the high traffic walking into his shop. He is talking to Dolphin, representing the Magical Kingdom Hotel owner, about renewing the lease agreement.

Only this time Dolphin did not have good news to share. The fame of the Magical Kingdom Hotel had spread across the entire galaxy, and generated lots of buzz from visitors across the universe. One of the most famous brands in the universe, known as Valiant Luxe (with the logo VL plastered on adoring fans' space bags), registered interest in taking up the space presently occupied by Rabbit's shop. Dolphin had courted the VL owners for many years, and finally got VL to sign an agreement to lease Rabbit's shop space at the Magical Kingdom Hotel.

VL's name would add tremendous prestige to the Hotel's branding and also attract other equally famous brands across the universe to set up shop in the Hotel. This would in turn increase the land, air, sea, and space traffic to the Magical Kingdom Hotel, boosting revenues and occupancy rates.

Dolphin thought of how to break the news gently to Rabbit, who had been a loyal tenant of the Magical Kingdom Hotel for the past 10 years. His quirky Rabbit T-shirts and hats had generated a loyal following amongst visitors. Now the shop looked worn and tired and in need of a major overhaul.

After exchanging pleasantries with Rabbit, Dolphin asked Rabbit what were his thoughts after occupying the space for 10 years. Rabbit recalled his early days as a struggling entrepreneur, and how Dolphin had taken a chance on him and offered him a space in a prime location to jump start his business. His business had really taken off since then and he was eternally grateful to Dolphin for her help and assistance all these years.

He did notice that the customer profile coming to his shop had changed.

Before, families would visit his store and buy lots of stuff from him, but recently he had noticed more visitors dressed in upmarket fashion wear and accessories. These new visitors had bought the more expensive accessories in his inventory, and ignored the goofy looking rabbit hats. He also noticed less families visiting his shop.

Rabbit lamented that his children were not keen to take over the running of his business, as they are all grown up and now working in jobs with prestigious sounding titles like Chief Space Officer, Master of the Universe, and so on.

Dolphin waited patiently for an opening to bring up the subject of a new tenant occupying the shop. She realized that Rabbit was getting on in years and had a hard time managing the large shop space and running the business with limited help and resources. She asked Rabbit, "If I could make a suggestion that would help you sell more to your new customers with less space and resources needed, would you like to know more?" Rabbit replied quizzically, "Of course, my dear. Go ahead. You were the one who gave me the opportunity to run my business in your prestigious hotel."

Dolphin replied. "I'm creating a new pop-up concept store where I allow you to sell your bestselling products from a much more compact space and you pay less rent. Plus you earn more profits because the store will still be in a good prime location and you need less staff. How does that sound to you?"

Rabbit replied, "Wonderful. But I'm still renting the current shop. My agreement runs out in a few more months."

Dolphin said, "Don't worry, I will take care of that. What you pay for the remaining term of the agreement will roll over to the new location. And I can offer you a 3-year term instead of the year-to-year agreement you have been leasing so far. Sound fair to you?"

Rabbit hopped with excitement. "Fantastic! You have always taken care of me and I'm sure you will continue to do so."

Moral: Take care of those who supported you in the past even as you achieve great success and fame.

Management Skill 6: Talk less, listen more, and ask the right questions. And make your customer an offer too good to refuse.

CHAPTER 7: HAVE AN INQUIRING MIND

Cat, the hotel manager, was discussing an exciting new business concept with a prospective partner Ms Cockatoo for a space in the Hotel's shopping arcade. Cockatoo wanted to sell different varieties of pre-packed bird seeds for visitors to buy and feed the different species of birds flying through the Magical Kingdom Hotel. She had observed that most visitors only gave one type of bird seed to all the birds. This is not ideal, as each species have their own specific dietary preferences.

So a sparrow and parrot have different dietary preferences. But how do visitors identify the species of birds and the appropriate type of food to feed them?

Cockatoo came up with a brilliant idea. Since all birds have an in-built tracking mechanism in their heads, where they remember where they came from even after travelling long distances to reach their destinations, she proposed using this homing mechanism to identify the bird species and its unique nutritional requirements. When the birds fly near to the Magical Kingdom Hotel, an alert is triggered to the visitors' virtual communication device (in this Universe there is no need to use a mobile phone to receive the alert, the alert is embedded in the visitors' minds). The visitor will instinctively know which type of bird is flying in and their preferred diet. And by simply thinking about it, it will trigger a signal which will send a message to the bird seed shop run by Cockatoo to prepare the right type of food for delivery to the visitor who requested it. Cockatoo was doing a roaring trade. Everyone loved her seeds.

This was the first time Cat had heard of such a brilliant idea. As far as Cat was concerned, he had not heard of such an idea being implemented in the rest of the Magical Animal Kingdom. He wanted to find out more about this idea. He knows his CEO, the mighty Lion, will not be happy if he did not do his due diligence.

So Cat prepared this list of questions to ask Cockatoo:

How do you ensure that there is no mix up in the order placed and the items delivered?

Cat knows the visiting birds are very vocal in their displeasure if they are not well treated. Eagle is constantly hovering in the air looking out for signs of complaints from his fellow birds, and he would swoop down to the Magical Kingdom Hotel and confront the Lion CEO directly.

How do you ensure that the communication device residing inside visitors' heads will work all the time? Any maintenance support provided? Will the device burst into flames if it is overheated through too much thinking? Does Cockatoo buy insurance cover for such eventualities?

Cat is curious as to what the answers might be. He stretched and licked his paws. It's been a long day. It's time for a walk in the beautiful garden and to chase some butterflies and fairies.

Moral: Be a Provider to everyone and your needs will be met.

Management Skill 7: You need to be curious, inquisitive, and ask many questions for ideas presented. Asking questions from the point of view of how to support the proposer in implementing the idea, what are the risks, and adopting risk mitigation strategies.

CHAPTER 8: DECISIVENESS

The Magical Kingdom Hotel had sent its talent scouts out on a recruitment exercise at the universities and colleges to get the best recruits to work at the hotel's new wing. Everyone at the Magical Kingdom Hotel is eagerly waiting for the opening of the hotel extension with its new Onsen suites with private Onsen bath, the beautifully furnished 5-star restaurant that serves mouth-watering street food from around the world at 6-star prices, and the latest trendy fashion accessories and jewellery store oozing with luxury from its every pore.

All except Snail, who is the Human Resource Director in charge of recruitment. A creature of habit, he moves very slowly and is not used to the fast-paced world of new hotel openings with large number of employees being recruited over a short period of time, to be on-boarded and trained to deliver perfect service from the word Go! on the first day of the hotel's opening.

Word got around to Mr Lion CEO that recruitment was being held back by Snail. Snail would sift through the applicants' resumes with a fine-toothed comb, looking for spelling errors, misplaced punctuation marks, and constantly seeking feedback from other department heads on the suitability of a candidate. This just would not do. The opening of the new wing was less than three months away and the mighty Lion was about to blow his top at the snail pace of staff recruitment.

Mr Lion CEO thought of the right person to do the job. "Hmm, let me place a call to Shark." Shark is a no-nonsense, sharp eyed problem solver with a sharp nose to sniff out trouble anywhere in the Magical Kingdom Hotel. Shark loves the smell of blood, the blood of the numerous candidates applying for jobs with the hotel.

While Snail is sifting through candidate number two's resume out of 1,000 applicants, Shark immediately zoomed in on the other candidates' applications. Shark is very decisive. Once he latches onto a suitable candidate, he does not let go until the candidate agrees to sign on.

Shark managed to recruit all the employees needed within three days. Snail was still looking at candidate number two's resume. When Shark reported back to Mr Lion CEO, Lion was impressed. Mr Lion is not easily impressed. When Mr Lion CEO commended Shark for a job well done, Shark replied, "You are most welcome Sir. Just give me more trouble to smell and I will be sure to lock my jaws onto the problem. Oops, I meant focus my mind to solve the problem, Sir." Shark grinned. He did not tell Mr Lion what he did to unsuitable candidates…

Moral: Slow and steady does not always win the race. Speed is of the essence.

Management Skill 8: In business, being decisive is key to making things happen. Nothing moves without a decision.

CHAPTER 9: WIN WITH STRATEGY

Remember the Rule of Three? Three competitors in the same location can triple your business. Ka-ching! How is this possible? Read on…

Eagle spied a wonderful location on the hotel grounds from the air. There was a fair going on run by the famous Ranco Brothers. They were doing very brisk business.

Eagle thought, "What if I place two other fairs together, each with their unique point of difference. Together with the Ranco Brothers Fair, it would attract a larger group of customers, and it would also drive more revenue for the Magical Kingdom Hotel."

Eagle swooped down to the owner of Ranco Brothers and told him his thoughts. Predictably the owner objected and felt his business will be affected with two other competitors located in the same area. Eagle explained that each fair has its respective strengths and attract its own crowd of customers. Eagle had already decided on this approach as he was very sure of his judgment. He convinced the owner to buy-in to his unusual business proposal.

After the other two fairs were started, business grew for all three fairs. The owner of Ranco Brothers admitted to Eagle that he was right after all. Eagle's long-ranging vision was proven right again. In the new world economy, it's about collaboration, not competition.

Moral: United we stand. Divided, we fall.

Management Skill 9: You need vision and strategy to see what others cannot see, and stand firm on your decision when you are sure you have a winning upper hand.

EPILOGUE – WHAT'S NEXT?

Dear Readers,

Have you encountered similar incidents in your career? Would you like to share how you resolved these issues? Tell your story using a fable, like what we did. The more fantastic your story, the easier it is to remember the principles.

We'd love to hear from you!

Visit our Facebook page at: fb.me/putthemagicbackintoyourbusiness or send a message to m.me/putthemagicbackintoyourbusiness. Tell your story in a minimum of 500 words. We'll publish the top nine entries with the most likes and comments as a sequel. The winners will each receive a complimentary e-book of the sequel, making your dream to be an author come true in the New Year!

Closing Date: Refer to Facebook page (conditions apply)

Put The Magic Back Into Your Business

ADULT COLORING PAGES

Have fun applying color to these pictures! Make your favorite character come to life!

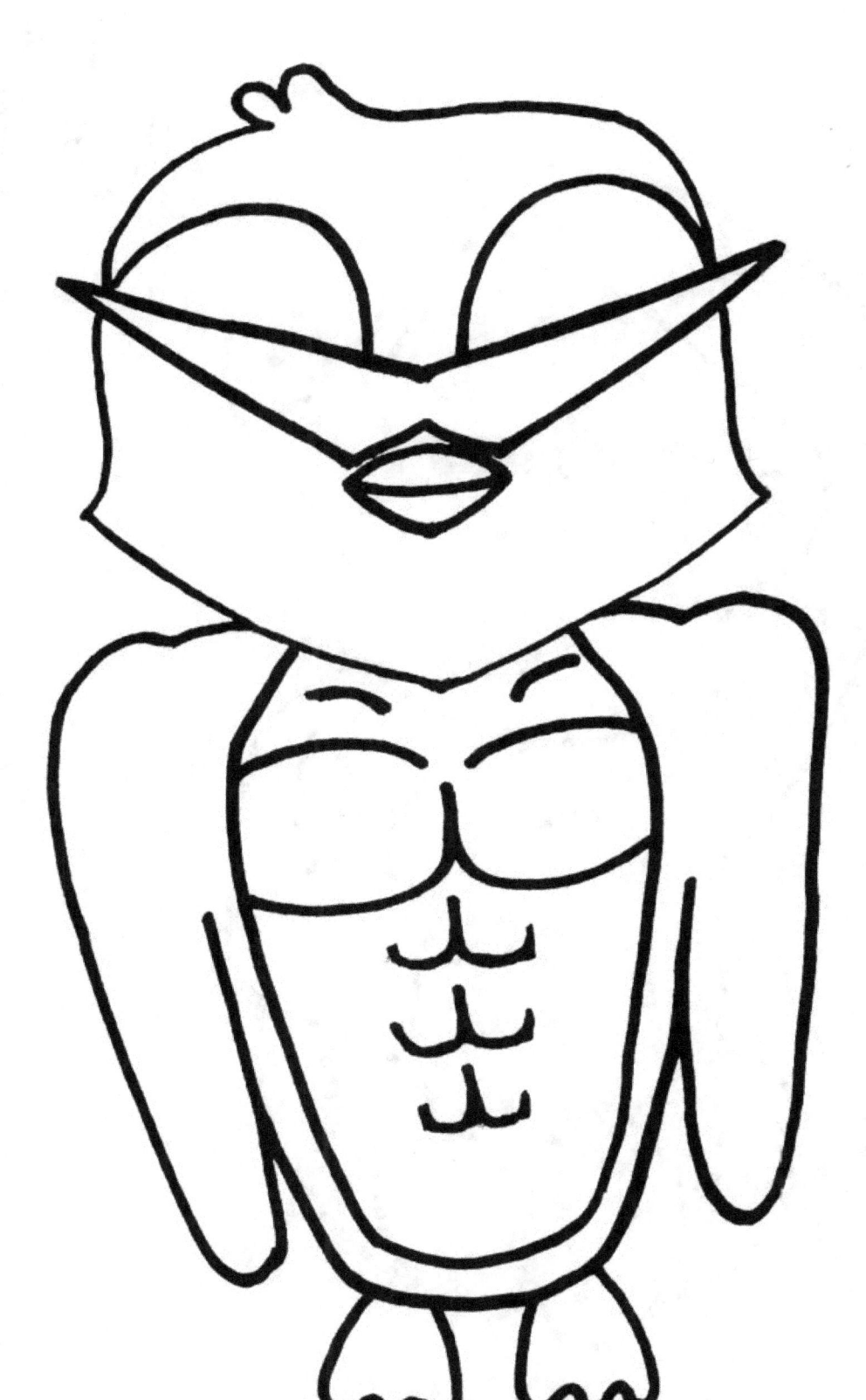

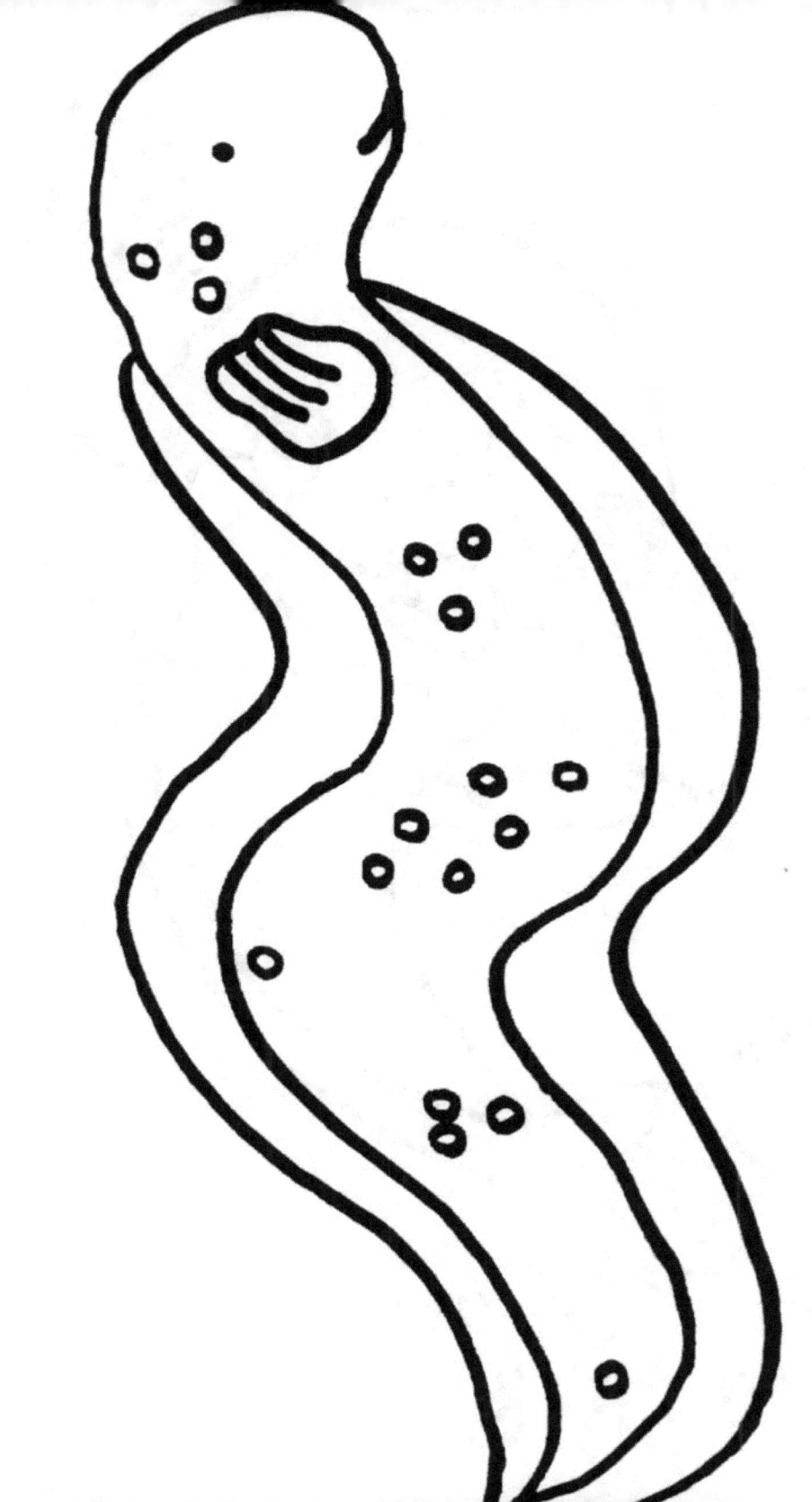

REFLECTION

REFLECTION

REFLECTION

ABOUT THE AUTHORS

Jih Min Cheng has held senior management roles in Retail Leasing, Mall Management, and Retail Development at many integrated property developments across South-East Asia for the past 30 years. He co-founded five businesses, and is presently a business adviser to several start-ups. He is Vistage Singapore Chair and CEO Coach, and a Member of the Singapore Institute of Directors.

He is actively involved in public speaking and leadership development at Agora Singapore Speakers Club and Association of Singapore Professional Speakers. He co-authored two books, Mystery Shopping and Stories of Aspiring Entrepreneurs. He holds an MBA from the University of Leicester, U.K., and a B.Sc. (Estate Management) degree from the National University of Singapore.

Jih Min lives in Singapore and travels around the region to network, identify market opportunities, and organize people and businesses to develop these opportunities.

Gracy Yap is a bestselling author (Kindle, Top 100 Paid) of several numerology books. She was featured in the press and TV in Singapore, Malaysia and Russian media. Gracy is a Cambridge certified teacher and a certified DISC Human Behavior Consultant. She has taught metaphysics classes in Singapore, Malaysia, Hong Kong, China, and now online to thousands of students from over 104 countries. She's also an ESL teacher to both young learners and adults. She lives in both Singapore and Malaysia with her crystal babies, and continues to write on subjects close to her heart.

www.ingramcontent.com/pod-product-compliance
Lightning Source LLC
Chambersburg PA
CBHW072239230526
45466CB00025B/2116